# AMERICAN QUILTER'S SOCIETY

AQS

# CATALOGUE
# of QUILTS

Located in Paducah, Kentucky, the American Quilter's Society (AQS) is dedicated to promoting the accomplishments of today's quilters. Through its publications and events, AQS strives to honor today's quiltmakers and their work and to inspire future creativity and innovation in quiltmaking.

EDITOR: BONNIE K. BROWNING
GRAPHIC DESIGN: KAY BLACKBURN SMITH
COVER DESIGN: MICHAEL BUCKINGHAM
PHOTOGRAPHY: SUPPLIED BY THE INDIVIDUAL QUILTMAKERS

Additional copies of this book may be ordered from the American Quilter's Society, PO Box 3290, Paducah, KY 42002-3290; 800-626-5420 (orders only please); or online at www.AQSquilt.com. For all other inquiries, call 270-898-7903.

Printed and Bound in Canada.

**W**ELCOME to the 19th Annual American Quilter's Society Show & Contest featuring the best of the best quilts from today's quiltmakers. We know that the quilts you see will inspire and challenge your creativity, and will awe you with their artistry.

Our goal is to help you thoroughly enjoy the show, and to that end this catalog of juried quilts was developed. Provided by the quiltmakers, these are the same photos our jury used to select quilts for participation in the contest. As with our contest, the catalog is divided by categories, and photos of the quilts are identified by title, size, and maker. For ease in finding your favorite quiltmaker's entry, an alphabetical index of quiltmakers begins on page 109.

To make the catalog easy to use, each new category is flagged with a colored AQS logo.

By turning a few pages you'll be able to see photos of the quilts in each category, and decide which ones you want to re-visit again in person. You may decide to use your catalog for notes, and possibly even autographs from winning quiltmakers.

Some of our guests may find this catalog will reduce their need to take as many photos of their favorite quilts – a definite plus in crowded aisles. We hope that long after you leave the show and Paducah, your memories of this year's show and contest will be enriched as you leaf through these pages. Thank you for joining us for the 19th annual AQS Quilt Show & Contest.

*Meredith Schroeder*

Meredith Schroeder
AQS President and Founder

**JAPANESE WATERBIRDS,** 69" x 81", LINDA F. DREYER, WHITEFISH, MT.

**A GIFT OF THE NILE,** 64" x 82", JUNKO YAMADA, NAGOYA AICHI, JAPAN.

**IN MY ELEMENT,** 84" x 92", GEORGE S. SHAFFER, NORTHUMBERLAND, PA.

**UNDER THE BOMBAX TREE,** 80" x 82", MASAKO KANDA, TOKYO, JAPAN.

**WINTER ROSES,** 75" x 90", NELL TOWNLEY, GOODVIEW, VA.

**WINDOW ON BEAUTIFUL KARUIZAWA,** 82" x 89",
SUMIKO MEGURO, TOKYO, JAPAN.

**KAHILI AND LEHUA,** 97" x 100", MARIKO TOMIZAWA,
YAMAGATA, JAPAN.

**APPLIQUÉ GARDEN,** 85" x 85", BARBARA DEETER,
SHREVEPORT, LA.

Patterns by Pat Andreatta from Heirloom Stitches 931-456-8584.

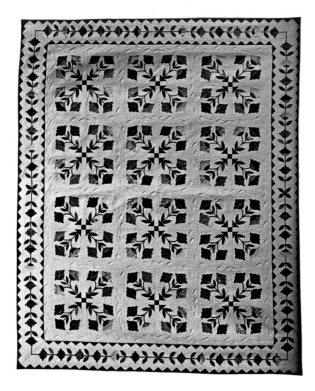

*Red & Green: An Appliqué Tradition by Jeana Kimball.*

**TIGER LILY,** 92" x 114", RUTH OHOL, LOCKPORT, NY.

**GARDEN OF RED AND GREEN,** 84" x 84", SHIRLEY GYLLECK, GENOA, IL.

**LOVE NEVER ENDS,** 92" x 92", LAHALA PHELPS, BONNEY LAKE, WA.

**KANOELANI QUILT,** 82" x 100", YOKO SAKAGUCHI, TOKYO, JAPAN.

*Red & Green: An Appliqué Tradition by Jeana Kimball.*

Permission to print quilt
not available at this time.

**SCENT OF INCENSE,** 73" x 80", MICHIKO SHIMA, NARA ,JAPAN

**ROSE LULLABY,** 72" x 84", NAOMI NAGAE, AICHI, JAPAN.

**BRIGHT HOPES,** 88" x 88", KAREN KAY BUCKLEY, CARLISLE, PA.

**CALIFORNIA BALTIMORE,** 79" x 91", SHIRLEY FLETCHER, ORANGE, CA.

**GOLDEN GLOW,** 88" x 88", MILDRED SORRELLS, MACOMB, IL.

**PHARAOH,** 76" x 82", SANDRA FRIEZE LEICHNER, ALBANY, OR.

**SECRETS OF THE DAYLILIES,** 67" x 80", J. PHIL BEAVER, FRENCH LICK, IN.

**AHINAHINA HALEAKALA,** 82" x 92", KATHY NAKAJIMA, TOKYO, JAPAN.

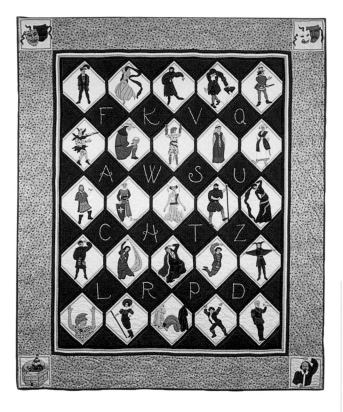

**I, OF THESE, WILL WREST AN ALPHABET,** 69" x 84",
PATTY ELWIN DAVIS, ITHACA, NY.

**FLUFFY FLOWERS,** 82" x 82", JULIE YAEGER LAMBERT,
ERLANGER, KY.

**GEORGE WASHINGTON'S REVENGE,** 88" x 88",
BETTY LU BRYDGES, VANCOUVER, BC, CANADA.

**FOUR EVER MORE,** 86" x 86", JUDI ROBB, MANHATTAN, KS.

*Magic Stack-n-Whack®, Bethany S. Reynolds, AQS.*

**AUTUMN FIREWORKS,** 83" x 83", JUDY VAN HOUTEN, NEW PALTZ, NY.

**BEYOND THE CENTURY,** 70" x 81", NORIKO KIDO, NAGOYA, JAPAN.

**DOUBLE WEDDING RING,** 88" x 98", SHARON BOWMAN, FORT WORTH, TX.

**LE MOYNE STAR,** 96" x 96", PATRICIA FEDERIGHI, SEATTLE, WA.

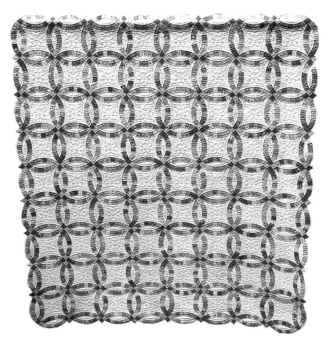

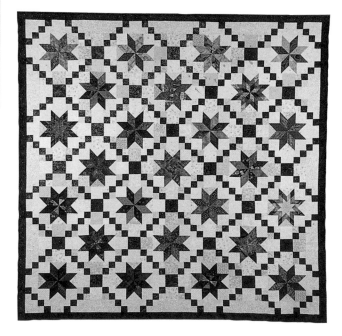

**BLUEBERRY MORNING,** 85" x 85", CYNTHIA SCHMITZ, ARLINGTON HEIGHTS, IL.

**STARRY PATH,** 88" x 88", CAROL DeFRANCE, TERRE HAUTE, IN.

**HARVEST TIME IN AUTUMN,** 62" x 80", TOMOKO ARAI, YAMAGATA, JAPAN.

**ATOMIC JUNCTION,** 110" x 95", MARION PERRAULT, BEACONSFIELD, QUEBEC, CANADA.

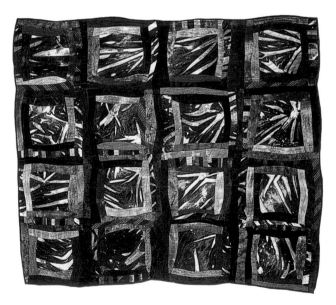

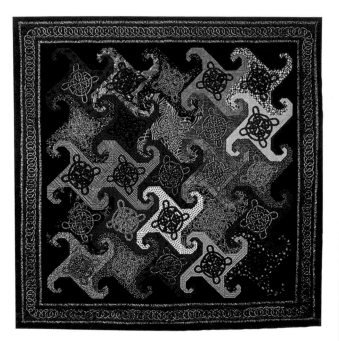

**STRIPES, DOTS AND FRIENDS,** 81" x 81", LUCY SILLIMAN, FORT SCOTT, KS.

**FULL CIRCLE,** 75" x 94", KATHRYN A. ASH, CHICAGO, IL.

**IN THE PINK,** 64" x 81", ANN HARPER, MONTGOMERY, AL.

**SOUTHBOUND,** 108" x 108", TRUDIE FAY, PHOENIX, AZ.

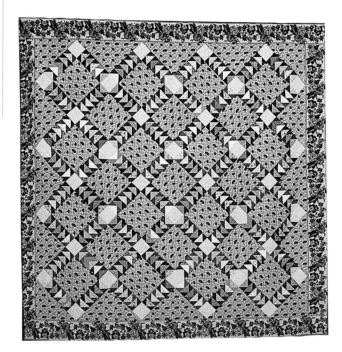

**PROMENADE,** 86" x 86", MICHIKO KONO,
HOJO, EHIME, JAPAN.

**DEAR JANE REVISITED,** 80" x 92", MARY SHARA, ATTICA, MI.

**BLUE LIGHT SPECIAL,** 82" x 82", JOYCE SAIA,
BEAUMONT, TX.

**INDECISION 2000,** 98" x 98", DIANNE RISSMAN,
POSTVILLE, IA.

**TEAPOT OBSESSION VIII: FAT FORTIES TEAPOTS WITH TEABAG SASHING,** 80" x 80", VIRGINIA ANDERSON, SHORELINE, WA.

**MANY STARS,** 86" x 86", NOBUE HAYAKAWA, NAGOYA-SHI, JAPAN.

**INTROSPECTIVELY HEXAGONAL,** 86" x 98", PAMELA A. DANESI, BROOKLYN, NY.

**NAVIGATING POINTS,** 88" x 100", FRAN KORDEK, ELKINS, WV.

400

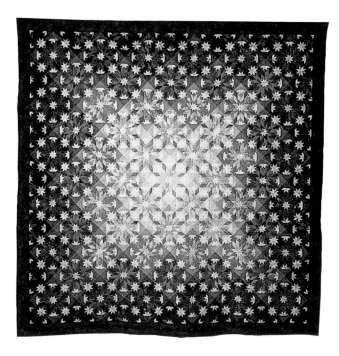

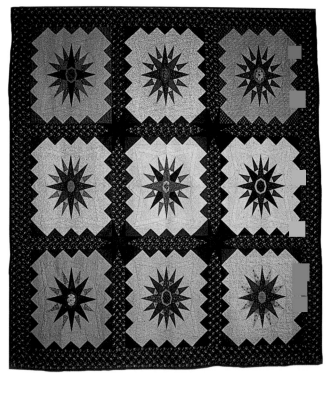

**SOUR CREAM AND CHIVES,** 67" x 82", CANDY GOFF, LOLO, MT.

**GALAXY,** 70" x 85", JANE HALL, RALEIGH, NC.

**LADY OF CRANE LAKE,** 83" x 93", SCOTT A. MURKIN, ASHEBORO, NC.

**SEW MANY SWIRLS,** 82" x 73", RENAE HADDADIN, SANDY, UT.

Prairie Star Basket block, ©Judy Martin, 1988. Used with permission.

**PRAIRIE STAR BASKETS,** 72" x 92", IRENE MUELLER, KIRKWOOD, MO.

**THE COLOR RUNS THROUGH IT,** 94" x 94", SUZANNE KISTLER, VISALIA, CA.

**WINTER'S BEAUTY,** 83" x 89", LORI MOUM, VIRGINIA BEACH, VA.

**NEW WORLD SYMPHONY,** 91" x 91", RICKY TIMS, ARVADA, CO.

**STANDING ON THE CORNER,** 75" x 88", JEANNETTE T. MUIR, MEDFORD, NJ.

**EMPTY NEST-TWO,** 85" x 93", BARBARA A. PERRIN, PULLMAN, MI.

**I'M IN LOVE WITH PERRY WINKLE,** 71" x 87", ELIZABETH SPANNRING, LA CENTER, WA.

**REFLECTIONS BEFORE THE FALL,** 67" x 84", SUE TURNQUIST, HARRISBURG, MO.

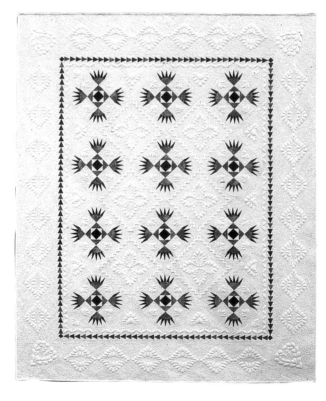

Pattern from *Quilts Galore*, Diana McClun & Laura Nownes, Walnut Creek, CA.

Design from *Travels with Peaky & Spike* by Doreen Speckman, C&T Publishing, 800-284-1114.

**LIBERTY STARS,** 87" x 87", BARBARA COPELAND, CULVER, OR.

**CAROUSEL,** 82" x 80", MARLA YEAGER, LITTLETON, CO.

**SUNSHINE FLOWERS,** 92" x 98", RUTH POWERS, CARBONDALE, KS.

**KIMONO,** 89" x 89", JANE FRENKE, BERKELEY SPRINGS, WV.

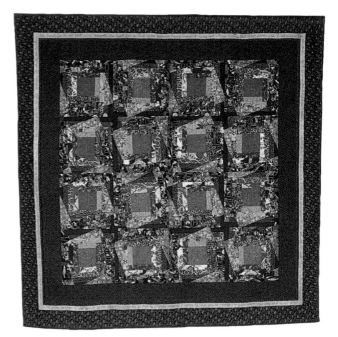

Permission to print quilt
not available at this time.

Permission to print quilt
not available at this time.

**IN THE PINK,** 79" x 99", JANE ANDERSON, VINITA, OK.

**THE NINES,** 96" x 96", PEGGY FETTERHOFF,
THE WOODLANDS, TX.

**BUTTERFLIES IN THE PEACEFUL FOREST,** 84" x 96",
RIEKO SANADA, FUJISAWA-CITY, JAPAN.

**MY BLUE FLOWER BED,** 74" x 91", DENISE L. CRAWFORD,
COTTAGE GROVE, OR.

Designs from *Wildflowers* by Carol Armstrong, C&T Publishing, 800-284-1114.

Appliqué pattern by Rose Hahn.

**THE DINER DECADE,** 69" x 86", MARY KAY MOUTON, MILLEDGEVILLE, GA.

**MY MOTHER'S GARDEN,** 83" x 87", SHARLENE JACKSON, WALDORF, MD.

**PADUCAH,** 75" x 90", YOSHIKO TAKAMURA, MATSUDO-CITY, JAPAN.

**NEW YORK BEAUTY,** 78" x 96", NELL TOWNLEY, GOODVIEW, VA.

Embroidered designs by Anita Shackelford. *Surface Textures.* AQS.

**FUNNY POND,** 70" x 90", HUNG-SOOK JANG, SEOUL, KOREA.

**MIDNIGHT BLOOMS,** 81" x 81", LINDA DYKEN, MOBILE, AL.

**GARDEN OF STARS,** 87" x 109", PATRICIA ROBERTSON, REEDLEY, CA.

**REINDEER MYSTERY,** 90" x 90", ERICA JARRETT, LIBERTYVILLE, IL.

**ORCHIDS,** 80" x 90", CHIZUKO HILL, TOKYO, JAPAN.

**ALL SEASONS,** 87" x 87", GWEN SPIESS, BRENHAM, TX.

**DEARLY SWEET VIOLETS,** 78" x 85", NAE IKEURA, OSAKA, JAPAN.

**PERENNIALLY YOURS,** 82" x 99", SHERRIE GROB, MURPHYSBORO, IL.

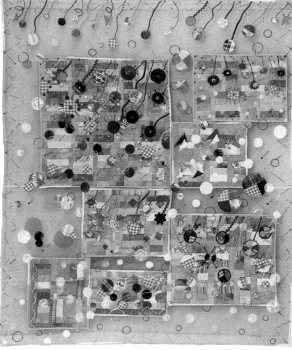

**DREAM,** 80" x 94", MELIHA TASKIN, ANKARA, TURKEY.

**BEING IN TENDERNESS,** 64" x 83", MASAKO KATOH, IBARAKI-KEN, JAPAN.

**A PICTURE OF HEAVEN,** 74" x 90", KUMIKO SATO, KANAGAWA, JAPAN.

**ROSE FANTASY,** 86" x 94", NORIKO UCHIDA, TOKYO, JAPAN.

Permission to print quilt
not available at this time.

**A SEASON OF HARVEST,** 80" x 80", KAZUE TAKAO,
UTSUNOMIYA, JAPAN.

**SPRING OF MOUNTAIN,** 92" x 81", MACHIKO YAMAMOTO,
PEORIA, IL.

**CLEOPATRA'S FAN,** 80" x 80", CONNIE RODMAN,
WEST FARGO, ND.

**IN CHANGING TIMES,** 82" x 82", SARAH FRANCIS,
GREENVILLE, TX.

Cleopatra's Fans by Tricia Lund & Judy Pollard, Classic Quilts. That Patchwork Place.

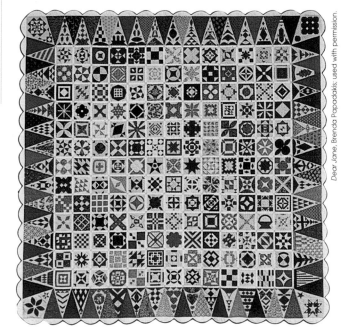

Dear Jane, Brenda Papadakis; used with permission.

**THE ALCHEMIST- STIRRING THE ELEMENTS,** 80" x 80",
BARBARA OLSON, BILLINGS, MT.

PATIO SCENE II, "SUNDAY"©, 78" x 87", JEAN M. EVANS,
MEDINA, OH.

**JUBILEE,** 79" x 80", LINDA McCUEAN, NEW GALILEE, PA.

HOT COTTON, 94" x 94", DIXIE HAYWOOD, PENSACOLA, FL.

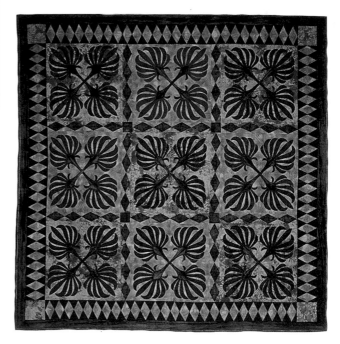

Adapted from Herbert Draper painting.

**A WATER BABY,** 82" x 86", CHRISTINE FRIES, BARRE, VT.

**FRENCH STARFLOWERS,** 75" x 89", JUDY MATHIESON, SEBASTOPOL, CA.

**SPRING SONG,** 88" x 89", SHIRLEY STUTZ, LORE CITY, OH.

**BOHEMIAN RHAPSODY,** 88" x 88", RICKY TIMS, ARVADA, CO.

**TO HAVE AND TO HOLD,** 67" x 83", JOAN ZEIER POOLE, SUN PRAIRIE, WI.

**MIDNIGHT IN THE GARDEN OF GOOD AND ELVIS II,** 81" x 81", ARLENE L. BLACKBURN, MILLINGTON, TN.

**FLOCKS OF FLOWERS,** 90" x 97", JOANIE WEEDEN, AUSTIN, TX.

**BLUE WILLOW AND GOOSEBERRIES,** 84" x 96", MARY KAY HORN, INDIANAPOLIS, IN.

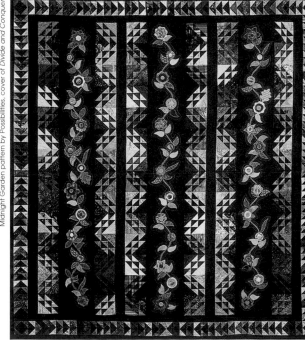

Midnight Garden pattern by Possibilities, cover of *Divide and Conquer.*

**BASKETS FROM YESTERYEAR,** 77" x 97", KIMBERLEE DIAMOND, COLUMBIA, MO.

**ICE CAVE,** 61" x 101", KATIE PASQUINI MASOPUST, SANTA FE, NM.

**FLOWER GARDEN,** 78" x 88", IKUKO NAGATA, COLUMBUS, OH.

**WILDLIFE,** 80" x 96", ELLEN HIGHSMITH SILVER, RYE, NY.

**A PERFECT MOMENT,** 85" x 101", SHARON SCHAMBER, JENSEN, UT.

**GEESE IN MY GARDEN,** 87" x 87", KATHY MUNKELWITZ, ISLE, MN.

**CELTIC GARDEN,** 95" x 100", MARLA YEAGER, LITTLETON, CO.

**ENDANGERED WARBLERS,** 76" x 81", GINNY ECKLEY, KINGWOOD, TX.

**SWEET PEA,** 86" x 86", CANDY GOFF, LOLO, MT.

**THE NUTCRACKER,** 67" x 82", KATHY McNEIL, MARYSVILLE, WA.

**TUNELESS RONDO,** 80" x 80", JUNKO SAWADA, YOKOHAMA, KANAGAWA, JAPAN.

**SAY IT WITH FLOWERS,** 74" x 95", ELIZABETH SPANNRING, LA CENTER, WA.

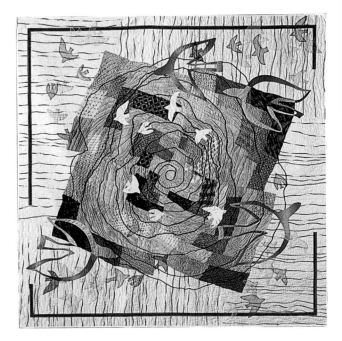

**LUSCIOUS LAVENDERS,** 98" x 98", SANDRA ESCONTRIAS, DELAND, FL.

**UALA - HAWAIIAN SWEET POTATO,** 80" x 80", LISA LOUISE ADAMS, VOLCANO, HI.

**BROKEN TIDDLY WINKS,** 62" x 83", DIANNE S. HIRE, NORTHPORT, ME.

**GENERA PLANTARUM,** 87" x 87", VIBEKE WILDER, LEE, MA.

Pattern from Piecemakers 2002 Calendar.

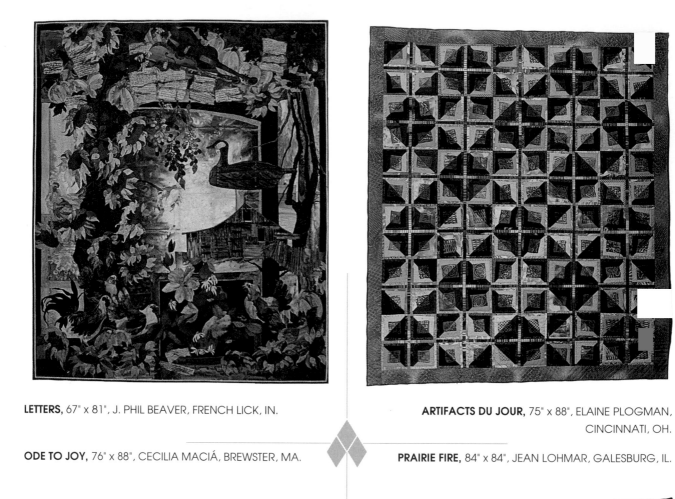

**LETTERS,** 67" x 81", J. PHIL BEAVER, FRENCH LICK, IN.

**ARTIFACTS DU JOUR,** 75" x 88", ELAINE PLOGMAN, CINCINNATI, OH.

**ODE TO JOY,** 76" x 88", CECILIA MACIÁ, BREWSTER, MA.

**PRAIRIE FIRE,** 84" x 84", JEAN LOHMAR, GALESBURG, IL.

**STAR FLOWER,** 83" x 83", ELSIE M. CAMPBELL, DODGE CITY, KS.

**TULIP TREE IN MAY,** 71" x 80", YOSHIKO KOBAYASHI, OSAKA, JAPAN.

**TEXAS TREASURES,** 47" x 64", SANDRA LARKIN DOUGLAS, McKINNEY, TX.

**BOUGAINVILLEA,** 83" x 83", BARBARA SWINEA, FAIRVIEW, NC.

**THE BEAUTY OF NEW YORK BLOOMS AGAIN,** 85" x 85",
PATRICIA DELANEY, ABINGTON, MA.

**THE EXPANDING UNIVERSE,** 98" x 98",
SARA M. SCHOENEBERGER, DALLAS, TX.

**MOONSHINE,** 97" x 94", CLAUDIA CLARK MYERS,
DULUTH, MN.

**ISIS,** 122" x 90" , GENE P. H. IVES, MELBOURNE, FL.

700

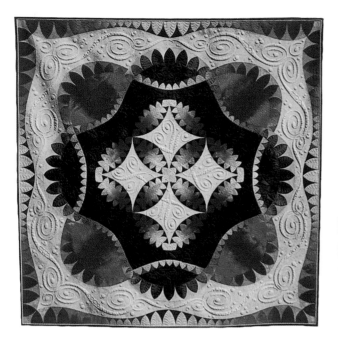

**LIME LIGHT,** 81" x 81", PHILIPPA NAYLOR, DHAHRAN, SAUDI ARABIA.

**BRILLIANT FUTURE,** 80" x 96", AKIKO SATO, TOCHIGI, JAPAN.

**NOSHIME,** 67" x 84", TOSHIKO TSUJI, OSAKA, JAPAN.

**NOWHERE FAST,** 86" x 86", PAULA PETERSON PLATTER, MEAD, OK.

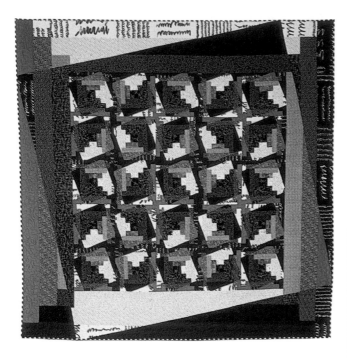

**STUDY IN BLACK AND WHITE,** 99" x 99", JANE FRENKE, BERKELEY SPRINGS, WV.

**RESERVED SEATING,** 72" x 85", MARTA AMUNDSON, RIVERTON, WY.

**SOLAR WIND,** 74" x 94", LUCY SILLIMAN, FORT SCOTT, KS.

**CALIFORNIA NITES,** 97" x 97", DERECK C. LOCKWOOD, CHICO, CA.

CRESCENDO, 67" x 86", CAROL TAYLOR, PITTSFORD, NY.

SUNFLOWERS, 92" x 92", CHRIS KLEPPE, MILWAUKEE, WI.

OUR CHILDREN OF FREEDOM, 91" x 85", SHARON SCHAMBER, JENSEN, UT.

FRACTURED FRACTAL, 71" x 87", JERRI STROUD, WEBSTER GROVES, MO.

Original design by Jerri Stroud, copyright 2003.

**FULL CIRCLE,** 83" x 83", BARBARA OLIVER HARTMAN, FLOWER MOUND, TX.

**SERENDIPITY,** 90" x 106", DEE MEYER, LAKE SAINT LOUIS, MO; QUILTED BY SHELLY McCLYMONT.

*800*

**MARGARET'S FLOWERS,** 84" x 102", MARGARET HOLLABAUGH, LOS ALAMOS, NM, & NICOLE DUNN.

**PROUD TO BE AMERICAN,** 109" x 86", KATHY EMMEL, ARVADA, CO, & THE 2001 6TH GRADE CLASS OF WEBER SCHOOL; QUILTED BY SANDY FRUEHLING.

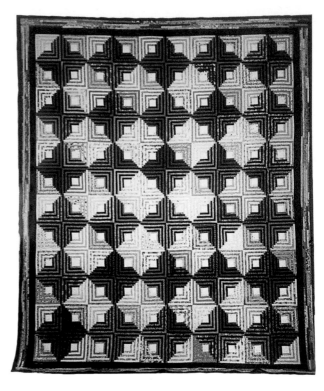

**BASKETS OF FRIENDS,** 82" x 101", ANN SARAH BROOKS, RICHARDSON, TX, & SCRAP BEE OF THE QUILT GUILD OF GREATER HOUSTON.

**SWEET POTATO PIE,** 69" x 82", SHELBY MORRIS, CARTERSVILLE, GA; QUILTED BY SUE HUNTSON.

**THE JUBILEE ALBUM QUILT,** 71" x 90", SUE NICKELS, ANN ARBOR, MI, & PAT HOLLY.

**RHAPSODY IN BLOOM,** 88" x 96", SHARLENE JACKSON, WALDORF, MD, BARBARA KOPF & LINDA SYVERSON.

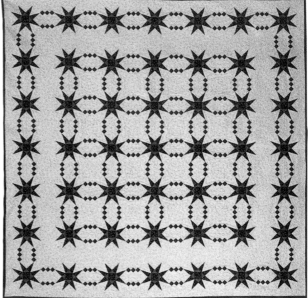

*Star pattern by Bob Coon, Quilted for Christmas II, That Patchwork Place.*

**CHRISTMAS POINSETTIAS,** 80" x 94", KAY & NORMAN COX, INDEPENDENCE, MO; QUILTED BY STOVER QUALITY QUILTING.

**TENNESSEE TWILIGHT,** 76" x 96", THE OUT OF TOWNERS, WHITE PINE, TN.

**RING AROUND THE STARS,** 86" x 86", JULIE KENNEDY, WAUWATOSA, WI; QUILTED BY JANICE L. WALSH.

**OHIO STAR ADVENTURE,** 84" x 107", CAROL L. STRONG, HARVEST, AL, THERESA FROGGE & ADA NEVILLE.

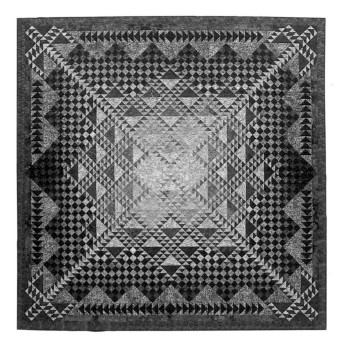

**TWILIGHT RENDEZVOUS,** 61" x 80", INGE MARDAL, CHANTILLY, FRANCE, & STEEN HOUGS.

**LADY OF 10,000 LAKES,** 99" x 99", CLAUDIA CLARK MYERS , DULUTH, MN; QUILTED BY KAREN McTAVISH.

**STARS & VINES 2002,** 88" x 88", KATHY DELANEY, OVERLAND PARK, KS, & CHARLOTTE GURWELL.

**NEW YORK BEAUTY IN LOUISIANA,** 90" x 90", BARBARA DEETER, SHREVEPORT, LA, & GAYLE WALLACE.

Pattern by Village Classics Patterns.

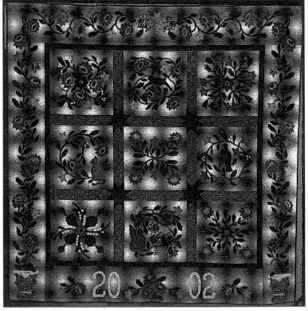

**CORN AND BEANS,** 104" x 80", LAURA FOGG, UKIAH, CA, & MEMBERS OF THE MENDOCINO QUILT ARTISTS GUILD.

**STACKED FEATHERS,** 96" x 105", SHARON SLIMMEN, HOLMEN, WI; QUILTED BY MEDNIS ENTERPRISES.

**VISUAL IMPACT,** 96" x 116", NORMA J. BARTON, ST LOUIS, MO, & MODESTA BASELER.

**BLOOMING NINE PATCH,** 89" x 99", PATRICIA C. KILMARK, ATLANTA, GA; QUILTED BY REGINA CARTER.

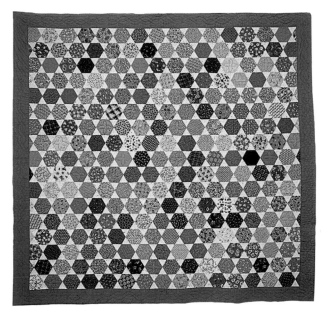

**STAR OF BETHLEHEM, GEORGIA,** 94" x 94", TERRI JARRETT, NICHOLSON, GA, PATTY TORNO, MARILYN OSTERA, MARY OLIVER, MARTY TANNER-HUGHES, SANDY JORDAN, MARY-BETH STALP & PRISCELLA GOLLEY.

**30'S I SPY,** 97" x 99", CLAUDIA NELSON, COLUMBIA, MO, & CONCORDIA CHURCH GROUP LADIES.

**FOUR PATCH FRIENDSHIP,** 100" x 104", ELIZABETH LORENZEN WILDEN, COLUMBIA, MO, SUSAN GILMORE, SARAH MAXWELL, & DELORES SMITH; QUILTED BY KIM DIAMOND.

**ROW HOUSES,** 74" x 96", RUTH POWERS, CARBONDALE, KS, ROSE WEIBE HAURY, JANE BUCKLEY, DENISE MAROLF, DEBBIE LILLICH, KATHY MAROLF & TAMMY OBLANDER.

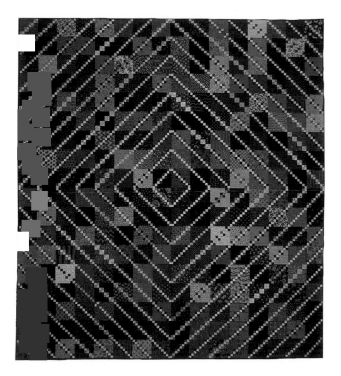

**FAN-DANGLE,** 78" x 94", JANET KNAPP, FERGUS FALLS, MN; QUILTED BY ROSALIE DAVENPORT.

**MARINER'S MOON,** 90" x 90", MARTHA GREENLY, ALLIANCE, OH, & JANET AMLIN.

**ELUSIVE,** 87" x 87", ELLEN GRAF, HAMILTON, OH, & LISA BONGEAN.

**TUSCANY,** 77" x 94", HILA LESLIE, RIO DE JANEIRO, BRAZIL; QUILTING DESIGN BY TONEE WHITE.

**SCREAMING PEACOCKS,** 81" x 81", LINDA V. TAYLOR, MELISSA, TX, & CHERI MEINEKE-JOHNSON.

**FLORAL COLLABORATION,** 96" x 96", ELISABETH POLENZ HAASE, SCHOFIELD, WI, & LUISE KRAMER POLENZ.

**CARDINALS IN THE COURTYARD,** 76" x 103", MARTHA ANN WARREN, EUREKA SPRINGS, AR, AUDREY HENDERSON & BARBARA SHANKS.

**CINDY'S BALTIMORE,** 96" x 96", CYNTHIA EGGERS, EAGLE RIVER, WI, & PAT BECK.

Original design by Jerri Stroud, copyright 2003.

Appliqué patterns by Dinah Jefferies, Garden City Gateworks.

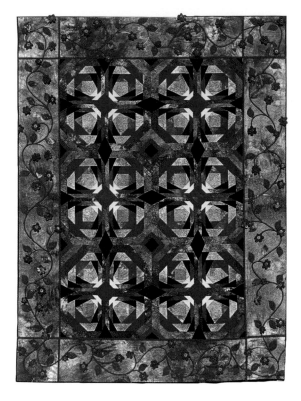

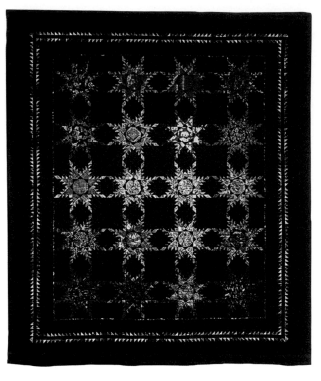

**JENNIFER'S QUILT,** 63" x 85", MARNI MacDONALD, SUN CITY WEST, AZ.

**FEATHERED STAR BEDSPREAD,** 86" x 100", LINNEA HIRST, DURHAM, NH.

**A PICNIC AMONG FLOWERS,** 83" x 90", EMIKO KAWABATA, TOKYO, JAPAN.

**WISH BIRD,** 82" x 90", LIUXIN NEWMAN, NORTH TURRAMURRA, NSW, AUSTRALIA.

Permission to print quilt
not available at this time.

*Pattern by Cynthia Tomaszewski/Simple Pleasures, Grand Rapids, MI.*

**THE SUN & MOON,** 77" x 85", BARBARA PERSING, FREDERICK, PA.

**KALEIDOSCOPE GARDEN,** 96" x 96", SANDRA M. SUTTON, SPRINGFIELD, MO.

**DRESSED TO THE NINES,** 91" x 100", CLAUDIA E. PEARCE, GLENWOOD, MD.

**ROSES ARE RED,** 88" x 90", SHERRY DURBIN, BURNSVILLE, NC.

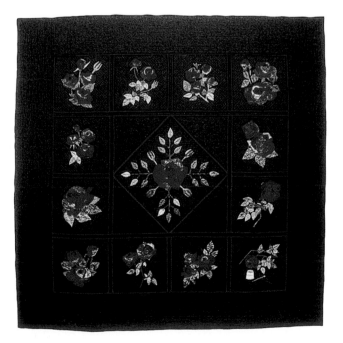

**MY FIRST SAMPLER,** 62" x 87", KYOKO KAWAI, TOKYO, JAPAN.

**CLASS OF '02,** 72" x 81", ALLEN DAY, WOLFE CITY, TX.

**THE ROWEL,** 65" x 88", HARUMI MORISHIMA, KOUTOUKU, TOKYOTO, JAPAN.

**FULL BLOOM ... A CELEBRATION OF 40,** 81" x 81", ANDREA M. BROKENSHIRE, ROUND ROCK, TX.

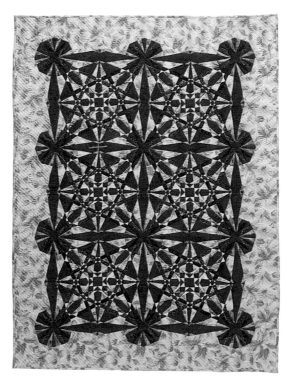

**WISTERIA ARBOR,** 92" x 92", PATRICIA ALFREDSON, ARLINGTON, VA.

**NEW ROAD,** 66" x 87", CHIEKO TERAJIMA, IBARAKI, JAPAN.

**GRANDFATHER'S GARDEN,** 85" x 108", MARGARET T. CACCAMO, NEW PALTZ, NY.

**COCHECO STAR OF BETHLEHEM,** 92" x 92", NANCY RINK, BAKERSFIELD. CA.

**STARS OVER AFRICA,** 69" x 87", MAGGIE EZELL,
SAN CLEMENTE, CA.

**MEMORIES OF LOVE,** 96"" x 96", DOLORES MEADOWS,
HARRISON, AR.

**BLESSING OF EARTH,** 81" x 81", UIKO ONUMA,
TOKYO, JAPAN.

**DREAMING OF SUN,** 100" x 100", MARINA KAMENSKAYA,
ARLINGTON HEIGHTS, IL.

Conway Album (I'm Not From Baltimore) pattern by Irma Gail Hatcher.

**BORN IN CONWAY – RAISED IN ST. LOUIS,** 95" x 95",
MARY ANN ANDERSON, FENTON, MO.

**FOR MY FAMILY,** 80" x 84", IKUKO HAGINO,
YOKOHAMA, JAPAN.

**SPIRIT,** 72" x 80", EunRYOUNG CHOI, SEOUL, KOREA.

**BE ENSLAVED BY THE MEDALLION,** 80" x 80",
KUMIKO KANAYA, HIGASHI-OSAKA-SHI, JAPAN.

**IDA'S DIARY,** 68" x 85", GAY S. BOWMAN, BELVEDERE, CA.

**HEAVENLY STAR,** 92" x 92", BONNIE ERICKSON, GRANITE FALLS, MN.

**AUTUMN LEAVES,** 85" x 85", MARIA DE GREENE, WOODLAND HILLS, CA.

**ORIENT OASIS,** 71" x 81", MASAE OBARA, TOKOROZAWA-CITY, JAPAN.

**LETTERS FOR LONG LIFE AND GOOD FORTUNE,** 80" x 90", SUN MI CHU, SEOUL, KOREA.

**A TINY TREASURE,** 23" x 23", BARBARA A. PERRIN, PULLMAN, MI.

1000

**SPIRALS IV,** 12" x 12", MARY M. BARNETT, RICHMOND, VA.

**MIDNIGHT BLOSSOM,** 14" x 23", ANNETTE M. HENDRICKS, GRAYSLAKE, IL.

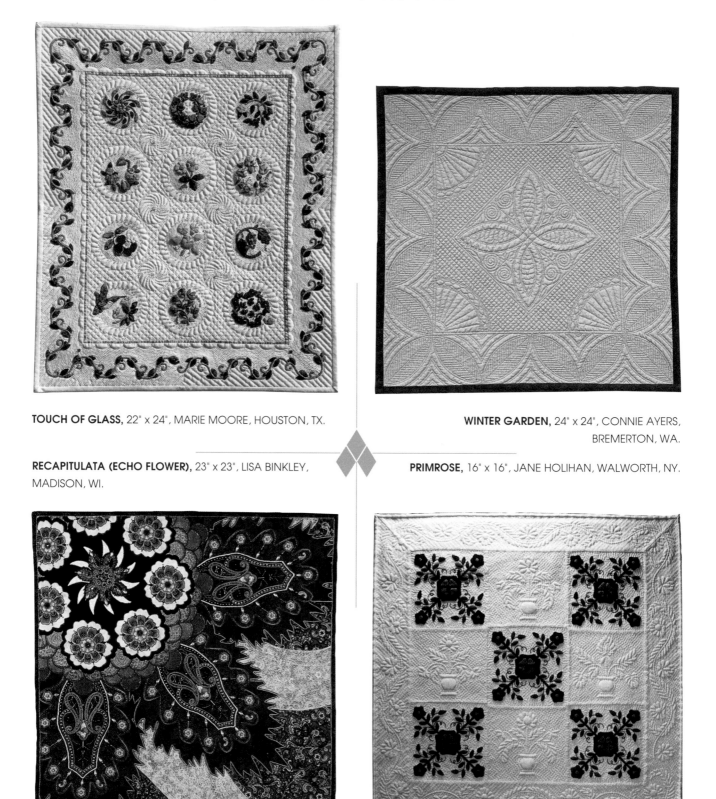

**TOUCH OF GLASS,** 22" x 24", MARIE MOORE, HOUSTON, TX.

**WINTER GARDEN,** 24" x 24", CONNIE AYERS, BREMERTON, WA.

**RECAPITULATA (ECHO FLOWER),** 23" x 23", LISA BINKLEY, MADISON, WI.

**PRIMROSE,** 16" x 16", JANE HOLIHAN, WALWORTH, NY.

**POT OF FLOWERS WITH BIRDS,** 11" x 13", PAT HOLLY, MUSKEGON, MI.

**PRINCESS FEATHERS,** 15" x 18", PAMELA HILL, QUEENSLAND, AUSTRALIA.

**COCHECO CHALLENGE 2002,** 13" x 13", RAINY STEVENS, LEBANON, ME.

**DANDELION,** 20" x 20", JANE MARIE ARUNS, ST. LOUIS, MO.

**HATTIE MAE,** 24" x 24", CYNTHIA JOHNSTONE, GREENVILLE, GA.

**ENIGMA 3,** 16" x 16", MARIYA WATERS, MELBOURNE, AUSTRALIA.

**PESKEY PINEAPPLE,** 17" x 19", MARLINE TURNER, PIETERMARITZBURG, SOUTH AFRICA.

**NINE TO FIVE,** 19" x 23", BARBARA ENGLER, BENTONVILLE, AR.

**THE CROWN JEWELS,** 13" x 13", JAYNETTE HUFF, CONWAY, AR.

**BUTTERFLIES,** 12" x 15", JUDITH DAY, LINDFIELD, NSW AUSTRALIA.

**WELCOME TO MY NEIGHBORHOOD,** 11" x 14", CONNIE CHUNN, WEBSTER GROVES, MO.

**STAMPEDE,** 18" x 18", PAT KROTH, VERONA, WI.

**MIXED MESSAGES,** 13" x 13", JOAN M. LADENDORF,
HANOVER PARK, IL.

**GREAT GRANDPA BROWN,** 20" x 24", NANCY S. BROWN,
OAKLAND, CA.

**LITTLE BITTY BALTIMORE,** 17" x 17", CINDY SEITZ-KRUG,
BAKERSFIELD, CA.

**LILIES AT NIGHT,** 14" x 14", DIANE BECKA,
NORTH BEND, WA.

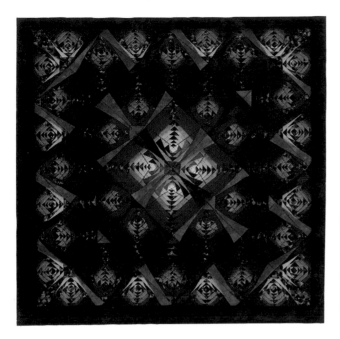

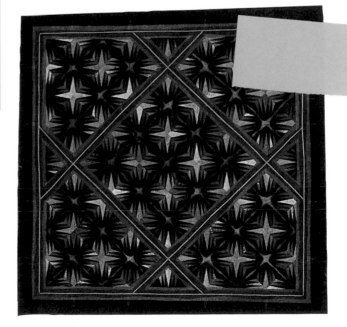

**PURPLE DAWN,** 11" x 11", GEORGE J. SICILIANO, CENTEREACH, NY.

**UNDER THE SUN FOR THE PEACE,** 68" x 69", NATSUMI OHARA, TOKYO, JAPAN.

**MY ALIEN GARDEN,** 63" x 77", SUSAN KNIGHT, BAY VILLAGE, OH.

**SHEER PLAY II,** 42" x 42", CLAIRE TEAGAN, HIGHLAND, MI.

**THE LIVE OAK,** 49" x 63", ANN SARAH BROOKS, RICHARDSON, TX.

**FRACTURED RIPPLES IN THE FABRIC OF LIFE,** 62" x 52", RITA STEFFENSON, EDWARDS, CA.

**BUGS 'N BUTTERFLIES,** 60" x 60", SHARYN COLE, SAMMAMISH, WA.

**GOING BEYOND,** 60" x 60", META MACLEAN, MONTREAL, CANADA.

*"Simple Gifts" pattern by Mary Sorensen.*

*Magic Stack-n-Whack®. Bethany S. Reynolds. AQS.*

Prickly Pear pattern by Karen K. Stone.

**LEARNING CURVES,** 55" x 55", SUSAN LIIMATTA HORN, SEA CLIFF, NY.

**SUNSET IN NEW YORK,** 63" x 75", HARUMI KANAYAMA, TOKYO, JAPAN.

**NEW DIRECTIONS,** 53" x 76, MARGARET T. CACCAMO, NEW PALTZ, NY.

**SHALLOW SEA,** 60" x 44", VIRGINIA ABRAMS, HOCKESSIN, DE.

**19TH ANNUAL AQS QUILT SHOW & CONTEST**

An Original Design by B.J. Titus. © 2003.

**NOCTURNAL SPONTANEITY,** 62" x 59", B. J. TITUS, COATESVILLE, PA.

**SINGING THE BLUES,** 63" x 76", KAYO MATSUO, NARA, JAPAN.

**THE WILD THING,** 74" x 74", KARLYN BUE LOHRENZ, BILLINGS, MT.

**ZINNIAS,** 44" x 44", BETH P. GILBERT, BUFFALO GROVE, IL.

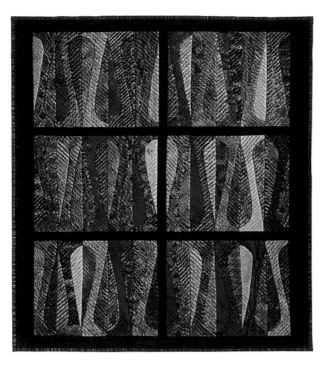

**FALL 2002,** 54" x 48", CHRISTINE A. MORGAN, PEQUEA, PA.

**MIDNIGHT BLOOMS,** 46" x 49", DONNA FORD, MADISON, WI.

**THE LAST SPRING,** 44" x 53", ANN FERKOVICH, SANTA FE, NM.

**GUSTAV'S TREE,** 40" x 44", ROSE K. OSTROVIC, CLEVELAND HEIGHTS, OH.

Adapted from Frank Loyd Wright design, *Liberty Magazine*.

**ALL WRIGHT,** 71" x 79", MAGGIE KOLVENBACH,
MT. KISCO, NY.

**SCRAPPY EAGLES,** 75" x 76", DOROTHY LeBOEUF,
ROGERS, AR.

**JUMP TO THE FUTURE,** 77" x 77", YONEKO MIZUNOE,
OITA PREF, JAPAN.

**ELVIS GOES TO HAWAII,** 64" x 64", BETH REISMAN,
NEWTON CENTRE, MA.

*Four Blocks Continued,* Linda Carlson, AQS.

*Appliqué patterns by Village Classics.*

**12 DAYS OF CHRISTMAS**, 55" x 59", CAROL G. BENSON, BARRINGTON HILLS, IL.

**SOMETHING CARRIED BY THE WIND**, 77" x 77", NORIE IRIE, SAKAI-CITY, OSAKA, JAPAN.

**THERE'S A BUG IN MY GARDEN**, 59" x 59", PAT KUMICICH, NAPLES, FL.

**CIRCLES VI**, 41" x 61", MARY M. BARNETT, RICHMOND, VA.

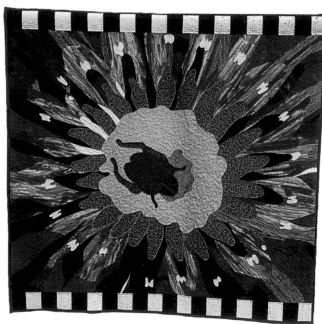

*Adapted from a photograph by Jonathan Blair, South African Monkey beetle and Gazenia bloom.*

**IN REMEMBRANCE OF NANNY,** 71" x 76", NANCY RINK, BAKERSFIELD, CA.

**SHADES OF GRAY,** 59" x 71", WENDY SLOTBOOM, SEATTLE, WA.

**A SPRING BREEZE OF RUNIUSGATAN,** 69" x 73", KATSUKO UDOH, TOKYO, JAPAN.

**IN THE DEEP FOREST,** 70" x 74", MIHO SHIMIZU, ABIKO-CITY, CHIBA, JAPAN.

**DAHLIA GRANDIFLORA,** 49" x 49", LISA BINKLEY, MADISON, WI.

**IT'S VERY GREEN,** 75" x 75", DONNA J. STEARNS, MANSFIELD, MA.

**WEDDING QUILT,** 53" x 59", ANIKO FEHER, OAK PARK, MI.

**FANTASY FLOWERS I,** 42" x 40", CATHERINE ERICKSON, WASHOUGAL, WA.

**CATHEDRAL,** 78" x 78", KAZUE TAKAO,
UTSUNOMIYA, JAPAN.

**FIESTA DEL MAR I,** 45" x 41", ANNE LULLIE,
LAKE IN THE HILLS, IL.

**"I-RIS-K" NOTHING,** 55" x 62", JOANNE WESTPHAL,
CHAPIN, SC.

**THE GARDEN,** 40" x 75", MARTI PLAGER, LOUISVILLE, KY.

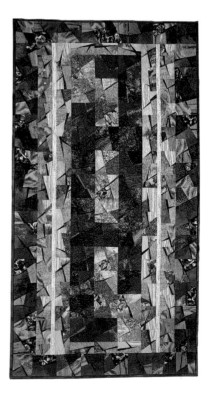

**GALA FIREWORKS,** 60" x 64", ETSUKO IITAKA, HIDAKA-CITY, JAPAN.

**BALTIMORE OCTAGONS,** 79" x 79", MARYN DeBOER, COLUMBUS, OH.

**EDITH'S LEGACY,** 52" x 67", PATTI ALLEN, FAIRFIELD BAY, AR.

**TULIPS INTO SPRING,** 48" x 51", SHEILA FINZER, ASTORIA, OR.

Prairie Calendar Sampler design by Prairie Star Quilts, Elk Horn, IA.

**IRENE'S GRAND ADVENTURE,** 58" x 71", VALERIE M. CHAPLA, PLEASANT HILL, CA.

**BLACKBERRY QUILT,** 64" x 64", LINDA FROST, LAWRENCE, KS.

**WHERE'S JOHNSON?,** 67" x 67", DIANE M. SEHORNE, ROUND ROCK, TX.

**NOCTURAL PINEAPPLES,** 73" x 73", ANNA FELL, GEORGETOWN, TX.

Samples from the Past, Blackbird Designs.

*Botanical Wreaths*, Laura Reinstatler, That Patchwork Place.

**LYN'S QUILT,** 53" x 53", JAN LEWIS, GRAND RAPIDS, MI.

**MY FLOWER GARDEN,** 62" x 62", FUMIE TANAKA, CHIGASAKI, KANAGAWAKEN, JAPAN

**TEXAS 2-STEP,** 58" x 58", ALICE PETRY-PREVOST, SAN ANTONIO, TX.

**A QUILTER'S GNOMES,** 60" x 69", ELNORA R. DYER, STAYTON, OR.

**PARTIAL CLEARING,** 43" x 43", JOAN M. LADENDORF, HANOVER PARK, IL.

**TUTTI-FRUITTI,** 54" x 54", VANYA NEER, BRADENTON, FL.

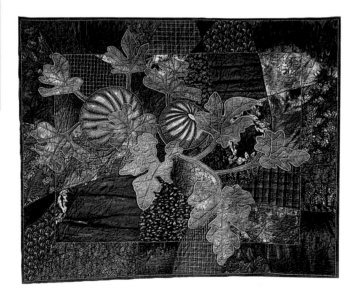

**GEORGANN'S BALTIMORE ALBUM,** 75" x 75", GEORGANN WRINKLE, HOUSTON, TX.

**THE PUMPKIN VINE,** 55" x 46, MARY-MARGARET MORTON, ANN ARBOR, MI.

Simply Delicious pattern, Piece 'O Cake.

SEASONS GO BY ..., 76" x 76", TAKAKO YAGI, TOKYO, JAPAN.

PRAIRIE STARFLOWERS, 67" x 67", MARTHA WALKER, PHOENIX, AZ.

BEHIND THE GARDEN WALL, 42" x 53", PAT DARIF, LOUISVILLE, KY.

GUARDIANS – CALL TO DUTY, 40" x 48", JOANN HALEY FARLEY, INDEPENDENCE, MO.

**I COULDN'T SLEEP AT ALL LAST NIGHT,** 50" x 65",
JANET SWISS, CARMEL, IN.

**AS SPRING UNFOLDS,** 65" x 65", ALICE GARRARD,
W. REDDING, CT.

**SHINING BRILLIANTLY,** 74" x 74", EMIKO KITANO,
OSAKA, JAPAN.

**HOME TOWN OF KAGUYAHIME,** 80" x 76",
KINUKO SAKURABA, TOKYO, JAPAN.

**TEXAS WILDFLOWERS,** 44" x 44", TERRI E. VOGDS, DENTON, TX.

**TEACUP,** 41" x 41", MARIA ELKINS, DAYTON, OH.

**BROKEN BOUNDARIES,** 62" x 63", CAROL TAYLOR, PITTSFORD, NY.

**SPANGLED STAR BANNER,** 56" x 80", SUSAN K. CLEVELAND, WEST CONCORD, MN.

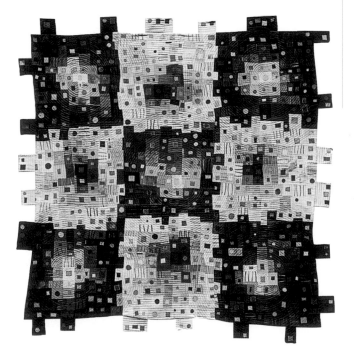

**IN MY GARDEN,** 52" x 60", SHARON CHENG, RICHLAND HILLS, TX.

**FLOWER GRAPHIX I,** 41" x 41", MARILYN GILLIS, SHELBURNE, VT.

**PESWARA,** 66" x 66", JEAN BIDDICK, TUCSON, AZ.

**HEAT WAVES III: INNER FIRE,** 57" x 58", LYNNE G. HARRILL, JESUP, GA.

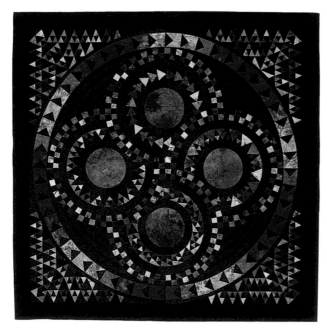

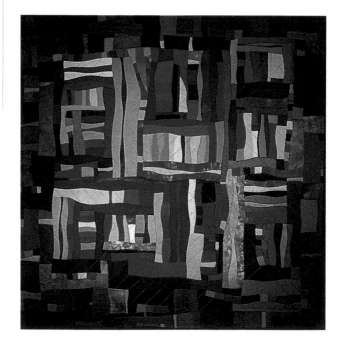

**DRAGONFLIES' DELIGHT,** 64" x 64", DIDI SALVATIERRA, BEL AIR, MD.

**TOTEM,** 62" x 50", GABRIELLE SWAIN, WATAUGA, TX.

**SPIN AROUND NEW YORK,** 41" x 41", GAYLE WALLACE, TAYLOR, LA.

**ON THE STREET WHERE YOU LIVE,** 48" x 56", JEANNETTE T. MUIR, MEDFORD, NJ.

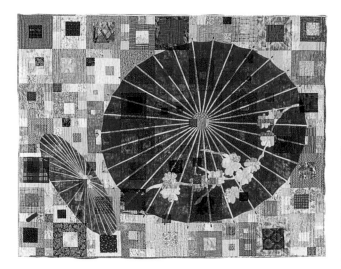

**XISHAUNGBANNA,** 71" x 56", MELODY CRUST, KENT, WA.

**IN THE GARDEN,** 42" x 53", MARLENE BROWN WOODFIELD, LaPORTE, IN.

**JOY,** 78" x 78", NANCY J. DUDLEY, WILSONVILLE, OR.

**PERSPECTIVES II,** 71" x 71", GLORIA HANSEN, HIGHTSTOWN, NJ.

**HOT HOUSE FLOWER: JUGGLING ACT,** 57" x 57". JERI RIGGS, DOBBS FERRY, NY.

**SOCIAL CLIMBERS,** 52" x 42", SUE HOLDAWAY-HEYS, ANN ARBOR, MI.

**LIGHT COMES SHINING THROUGH,** 43" x 43", LYN D. JOHNSON, COLUMBIA, SC.

**SINGLE WATER LILY,** 55" x 47", ANN FAHL, RACINE, WI.

**SUMMER IN A SHADE GARDEN,** 59" x 62", JO DIGGS, PORTLAND, ME.

**APPROACHING EQUINOX,** 56" x 53", CAROL SODERLUND, GENEVA, NY.

**TRELLIS OF ROSES,** 77" x 77", JANICE MADDOX, ASHEVILLE, NC.

**THE WISE AND FOOLISH VIRGINS,** 47" x 57", SUZANNE MARSHALL, CLAYTON, MO.

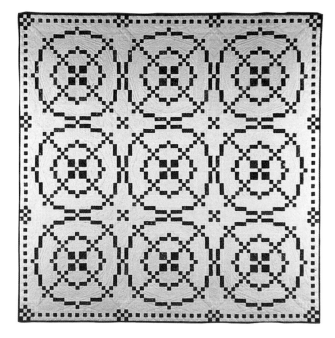

**KALAHARI DREAMING,** 41" x 56", JO BARRY, PORTLAND, OR.

**BLOOM BY BLOOM COMES THE SUMMER,** 77" x 50", JUANITA YEAGER, LOUISVILLE, KY.

**EARTH QUILT #98: LINES XVI,** 67" x 69", MEINY VERMAAS- van der HEIDE, TEMPE, AZ.

**MIDNIGHT STAR,** 45" x 45", SHERRI BAIN DRIVER, CENTENNIAL, CO.

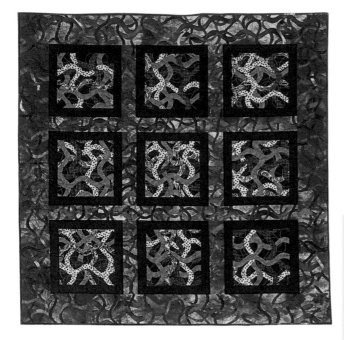

**THINKING OUTSIDE THE BOX,** 60" x 60",
ARLENE L. BLACKBURN, MILLINGTON, TN.

**PAISLEY PROPELLER,** 63" x 63", MARY MASHUTA,
BERKELEY, CA.

**SEEDLINGS,** 53" x 43", MICKEY DEPRE, OAK LAWN, IL.

**SPIROGYRA,** 44" x 65", CARYL BRYER FALLERT,
OSWEGO, IL.

*Roots, Feathers, and Blooms, Linda Carlson, AQS.*

**FEATHERS FROM AN EMPTY NEST,** 62" x 62",
LINDA CRAGG BUZON, SAGINAW, MI.

**IT'S ABOUT TIME,** 52" x 67", JANET STEADMAN, CLINTON, WA.

**MOONDANCE,** 47" x 40", MICHELE HARDY, MANDEVILLE, LA.

**SUNFLOWER,** 48" x 48", SHERRI L. TUREVON, McKINNEY, TX.

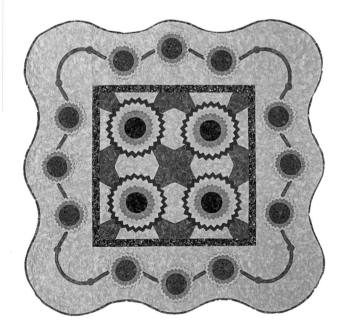

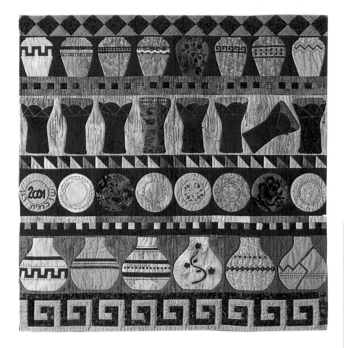

**BAZAAR RHYTHM,** 48" x 48", SHULAMIT RON, KADIMA, ISRAEL.

**HOPE FLOURISHES,** 66" x 66", RACHEL A. WETZLER, ST. CHARLES, IL.

**ADIOS AMIGOS, HOLA MEXICO,** 59" x 52", MARTA AMUNDSON, RIVERTON, WY.

**STRING THEORY,** 43" x 56", ROBBI JOY EKLOW, THIRD LAKE, IL.

**FLORAL FANTASY #3: NIGHT BLOOMING CABIN FLOWER,** 79" x 79", SUE TURNQUIST, HARRISBURG, MO.

**HUNGRY?,** 53" x 69", IRENE MUELLER, KIRKWOOD, MO.

**ALL JOIN HANDS,** 49" x 49", ELAINE PLOGMAN, CINCINNATI, OH.

**BUTTERFLY GARDEN,** 63" x 47", CINDY VOUGH, NICHOLASVILLE, KY.

Simply Delicious pattern by Piece 'O Cake.

**ANOTHER BLUE PLATE SPECIAL,** 41" x 44", SANDRA SMART, RICHLAND, WA.

**SOLUS,** 57" x 57", ISABEL SCHNEIDER, HAUTERIVE, SWITZERLAND.

**WELSH DRESSER,** 67" x 53", GWENFAI REES GRIFFITHS, NORTH WALES, UK.

**FLOWER BEDS AT TWILIGHT,** 42" x 47", SALLY K. FIELD, HAMPDEN, ME.

"Water Lilies" designed by Aie Rossmann, Lotusland's Appliqué Patterns.

**WATER LILIES,** 65" x 65", MARY K. REED, JONESBORO, IL.

**SUMMER SONG IN SIX,** 62" x 62", KATHLEEN SNYDER, NISKAYUNA, NY.

**DOLPHIN WAVES,** 71" x 72", LISA LOUISE ADAMS, VOLCANO, HI.

**CUTTING CORNERS,** 59" x 65", BARBARA BARRICK McKIE, LYME, CT.

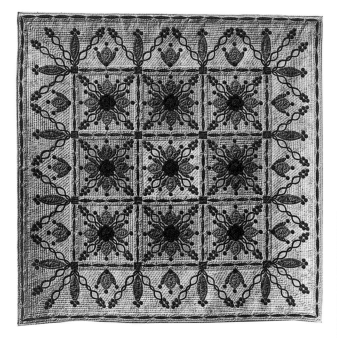

**CRISS-CROSSED CONNECTIONS,** 62" x 62", LINDA M. ROY, PITTSFIELD, MA.

**CORAL ISLAND,** 76" x 76", KAZUKO FUNABASAMA, GUNMA, JAPAN.

**SIERRA SUNRISE,** 78" x 78", MARGARETE C. HEINISCH, WEST HILLS, CA.

**MATTIE'S LEGACY,** 47" x 54", KATHY EMMEL, ARVADA, CO.

**ARKANSAS FLORAE,** 63" x 63", MARIE HENRY,
LITTLE ROCK, AR.

**SUNFLOWERS IN AUGUST,** 43" x 45", FRIEDA L. ANDERSON,
ELGIN, IL

**HIDDEN STARS,** 55" x 55", JOANNE B. MYERS, BEND, OR.

**A LONE RIDER,** 56" x 50", KATIE VACLAVIK, PLATTEVILLE, WI.

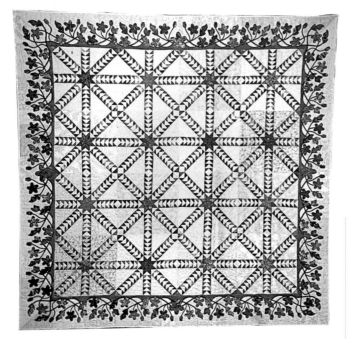

**ARACHNE,** 75" x 75", PAULETTE PETERS, ELKHORN, NE.

**GINGER FLOWER AT SUNSET,** 70" x 76", KATHY NAKAJIMA,
TOKYO, JAPAN.

**BULL'S EYE,** 47" x 47", SUZANNE MUSE TAYLOR,
SAN DIEGO, CA.

**A TOUCH OF YELLOW,** 72" x 74", CAROL A. SELEPEC,
MIDLAND, PA.

**JIGSAW GIANTS,** 50" x 74", CASSANDRA WILLIAMS, GRANTS PASS. OR.

**AFTER THE RAIN,** 53" x 63", MARY L. HACKETT, CARTERVILLE, IL.

**LUNACY IV: THE WEIGHT OF THE EVIDENCE,** 49" x 57", VALERIE M. CHAPLA, PLEASANT HILL, CA.

**PINK DOGWOODS,** 40" x 47", PAT BLANKENSHIP, KNOXVILLE, TN.

**FLOWERS OF THE CROWN,** 78" x 58", SHIRLEY P. KELLY, COLDEN, NY.

**WASHINGTON, D.C.,** 56" x 59", ELIZABETH ALOFS, LAKESIDE, CA.

**THE WILD GARDEN - SUNDOWN,** 64" x 46", RITA STEFFENSON, EDWARDS, CA.

**HEMEROCALLIS - DAYLILY,** 44" x 50", PAM MORAN, PLYMOUTH, MN.

**ATTITUDES,** 66" x 43", CYNTHIA JOHNSTONE, GREENVILLE, GA.

**GARDEN SERENADE,** 57" x 65", MICKEY DEPRE, OAK LAWN, IL.

**THE APARTMENT,** 59" x 78", LINDA CANTRELL, ASHEVILLE, NC.

**RAY'S HOPE,** 72" x 53", KAZUKO COVINGTON, GALENA, OH.

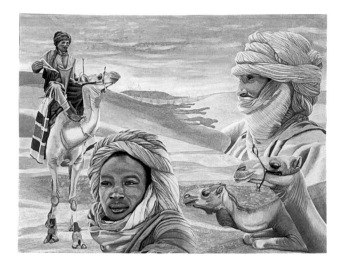

**BLUE MEN,** 78" x 60", HOLLIS CHATELAIN, HILLSBOROUGH, NC.

**MACROCARPA AND FRIENDS,** 75" x 75", SUSAN MATHEWS, YARRAWONGA, VICTORIA AUSTRALIA.

**BIG RIVER HERON,** 60" x 51", LAURA FOGG, UKIAH, CA.

**THE CAPTAIN'S WIFE,** 58" x 80", HELENE KNOTT, OREGON CITY, OR.

**RED STAR AMARYLLIS,** 46" x 42", BARBARA BARRICK McKIE, LYME, CT.

**NOT WRITTEN IN STONE,** 42" x 54", ESTERITA AUSTIN, PORT JEFFERSON STATION, NY.

**OLYMPIC TRIBUTE,** 56" x 43", LINDA S. SCHMIDT, DUBLIN, CA.

**LIVE OAK,** 45" x 41", SANDY BOSLEY, BOTHELL, WA.

Adapted from a photograph by Treat Nelson, Salt Lake City, UT.

S. W. Bosley © 2002.

**WALKS IN THE WOODS,** 65" x 57", FRIEDA ANDERSON,
ELGIN, IL.

**PEARL OF HOLLAND,** 60" x 48", PAT BUSBY,
LAKE OSWEGO, OR.

**ASPENS ALONG THE SNAKE RIVER,** 59" x 44", CATHY GEIER,
WAUKESHA, WI.

**iCANDY,** 56" x 69", ROBBI JOY EKLOW, THIRD LAKE, IL.

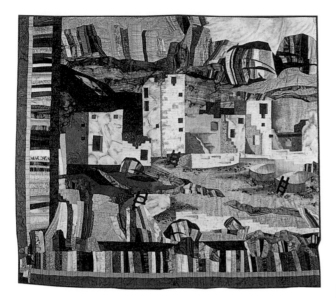

**MESA VERDE,** 63" x 57", SUZANNE MUSE TAYLOR, SAN DIEGO, CA.

**FROM WHENCE WE CAME TO WHERE WE GO,** 54" x 53", DENISE TALLON HAVLAN, PALOS HILLS, IL.

**SHAKE A LEG,** 57" x 41", CAROL GODDU, ONTARIO, CANADA.

**GOLDIE,** 43" x 56", ANIKO FEHER, OAK PARK, MI.

**NATIVE LANDS,** 51" x 44", GINNY ECKLEY, KINGWOOD, TX.

**THE RED PAGODA,** 57" x 71", SUE GILGEN, MADISON, WI.

**SOMETHING TO CROW ABOUT,** 46" x 52", HARRIETTE JANKE, MANHATTAN, KS.

**REALLY RED FLOWERS,** 40" x 67", KAREN R. PEDERSON, SEATTLE, WA.

A Country Journal, Maggie Walker Design.

**POLAR PROWLER,** 51" x 71", PATRICIA M. GOFFETTE, EDMONDS, WA.

**FLAMING AZALEAS,** 53" x 42", MARLENE BROWN WOODFIELD, LA PORTE, IN.

**DANCING PEACE,** 69" x 61", LURA SCHWARZ SMITH, COARSEGOLD, CA.

**LITTLE VENICE, MYKONOS, GREECE,** 58" x 52", BETTY BLAIS, TIGARD, OR.

**END OF THE SEASON,** 48" x 48", ANN FAHL, RACINE, WI.

**QUILT FAIRY - A SELF PORTRAIT,** 44" x 69", KAREN HULL SIENK, COLDEN, NY.

**DARE TO DREAM,** 51" x 69", SHARON MALEC, WEST CHICAGO, IL.

**A MIDSUMMER'S DAYDREAM,** 54" x 57", NATALIA MANLEY, LONDON, UNITED KINGDOM.

**QUILT SHOW AT RIVER DANIEL FARM,** 51" x 41", MARY ABBOTT WILLIAMS. PINEHURST, NC.

**BIRD OF HOPE,** 48" x 48", BARBARA LYDECKER CRANE, LEXINGTON, MA.

**THE NIEBUR SISTERS,** 52" x 46", NANCY S. BROWN, OAKLAND, CA.

**SPRING FEVER,** 61" x 51", STACIE MANN. LEE, ME.

**HIDDEN VALLEY,** 50" x 49", KATIE VACLAVIK, PLATTEVILLE, WI.

**BUTTON WEED #2,** 55" x 69", CARYL BRYER FALLERT, OSWEGO, IL.

**UNDERFOOT,** 68" x 60", CORINE BUECHNER, MARCELL, MN.

**TANGLEWOOD DRIVE,** 58" x 47", ESTELLE PORTER, ASHLAND, VA.

**BIRCHES,** 77" x 50", NATALIE SEWELL, MADISON, WI.

**DÉJÀ VU,** 60" x 61", MARY MANAHAN, NEWTOWN, PA.

**FARMER IN THE DELL,** 48" x 67", JOANNE GASPERIK, ST. JAMES CITY, FL.

**SERENITY,** 71" x 50", KATHY McNEIL, MARYSVILLE, WA.

**MORNING GLORY,** 64" x 68", JUANITA YEAGER, LOUISVILLE, KY.

**WE'RE NOT IN KANSAS ANYMORE,** 66" x 66", KARLYN BUE LOHRENZ, BILLINGS, MT.

**COUNTRY ROADS,** 60" x 44", NANCY PRINCE, OVIEDO, FL.

**'52 PICKUP,** 61" x 42", MARCIA STEIN, SAN FRANCISCO, CA.

**AUTUMN WOODS,** 72" x 54", SUE GILGEN, MADISON, WI.

**TOWARDS THE LIGHT,** 57" x 41", PAMELA DRUHEN, NORTHFIELD, VT.

1400

**HE'S COME UNDONE,** 59" x 80", LINDA GILLESPIE, BATTLE CREEK, MI, CATHY ZANONI, REBECCA KELLEY.

**MANDALA I,** 58" x 58", JERI RIGGS, DOBBS FERRY, NY, & TOM DILELLO.

**GARDEN SAMPLER,** 72 x 72", ANJA TOWNROW, WALSALL, UK, & JACKIE TONKS.

**QUILT OF MANY COLORS,** 75" x 75", BARBARA SHOPHER, CONCORD, CA, & NINA FARRELL.

**LOON REE-DESIGNED,** 63" x 46", DENALI QUILTERS, DENALI PARK, AK; QUILTED BY REE NANCARROW.

**THE GARDEN GATE,** 60" x 63", NATALIE SEWELL, MADISON, WI, & NANCY ZIEMAN.

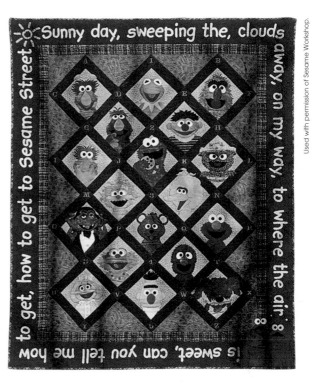

Used with permission of Sesame Workshop.

**BEYOND DESTINY,** 71 x 56", INGE MARDAL, CHANTILLY, FRANCE & STEEN HOUGS.

**SESAME STREET,** 55" x 68", LISA BUNESCU, CAMBRIDGE, WI; QUILTED BY PATCHWORK PEDDLER.

**DANCING IN THE DARK,** 62" x 80", SHIRLEY STUTZ, LORE CITY, OH, & VICKIE YANIK.

**VORTEX,** 68" x 70", FAY PRITTS & MERL PRITTS, MT. PLEASANT, PA.

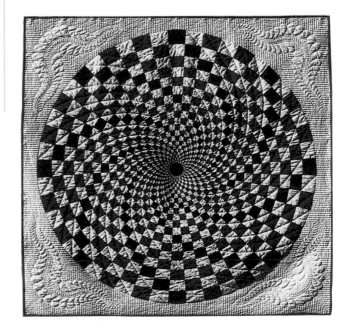

**THE CHIMNEYS - GREAT SMOKY MOUNTAINS NATIONAL PARK,** 53" x 70", BARBARA WEBSTER, BURNSVILLE, NC; SHERRY DURBIN & RACHEL REESE.

**THROUGH THE TURNSTILES,** 56" x 76", MARCIA HANDSAKER, NEVADA, IA, & MIRIAM BEAMAN.

**PARADOSSO (PARADOX),** 59" x 74", DOROTHY M. BRINKMAN, ARKANSAS CITY, KS. & SUZANNE W. BROWN.

**UNLIMITED COURAGE - UNCONDITIONAL LOVE,** 60" x 72", WENDY S. FOIST, GRANBURY, TX, & KATHY OLSON.

# Quilt Contest Rules

1. Anyone can enter a cloth quilt by submitting entry blank, entry fee, and slides of the completed work.
2. Quilt must be constructed and quilted by person(s) named on entry blank.
3. All quilt entries are to be completely stitched by one person except in the Group categories #8 and #14.
4. All quilts must be quilted by hand, by machine, or both.
5. Quilt entries will be considered for Hancock's Best of Show, Hand Workmanship, Bernina Machine Workmanship & RJR Best Wall Quilt purchase awards. Winners in these four divisions not wishing to relinquish their quilts may retain possession of their quilts by refusing their prize money. Photographing and printing rights must still be granted to AQS.
6. Quilt must have been finished after 2001 and be in excellent condition.
7. Quilts displayed in previous AQS shows or made from pre-cut or stamped kits are ineligible.
8. Limit **two** entries per person, *one quilt per category.*
9. Quilts in categories 1 – 9 must be at least 60 inches across (110" maximum) and at least 80 inches long or larger.
10. Wall quilts, categories 11 – 14, must be minimum size 40 inches x 40 inches; maximum size 80 inches x 80 inches.
11. Miniature quilts (category 10) can use any technique; maximum size 24 inches x 24 inches.
12. Quilts must be a single unit and not framed with wood, metal, etc.
13. Quilts that combine two or more techniques (other than quilting) should be entered in the Mixed Techniques category (i.e., piecing and appliqué, appliqué and embroidery, etc.)
14. Quilts in category 9 must be a first-time entry by an **amateur** in the AQS contest.
15. Full-view slide must show all edges of the finished quilt. Detail slide must show the quilting stitches. Please do not send glass slides.
16. Quilt must be available for judging and display from April 9 through April 30, 2003.
17. Incomplete, torn, or soiled quilts will not qualify for entry or exhibition.
18. All decisions of the jurors and judges are final. AQS reserves the right to reject any entry, including those that fail to follow the quilt contest rules.
19. Please include the complete name and address of your local newspaper so a news release can be mailed there.

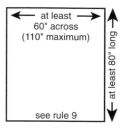

To Enter, Send:
- (a) Completed and signed entry blank with correct category circled
- (b) Two 35mm slides only (1 full-view and 1 close-up of completed quilt)
- (c) AQS members $5.00 entry fee per quilt
    Non-members $25.00 entry fee per quilt

# Timetable

| January 2, 2004 | Slides, entry blank, and entry fee must be received by AQS, or postmarked, no later than January 2, 2004. Slides of quilts accepted for competition will not be returned. |
| March 5, 2004 | All entrants will be notified. If your quilt is accepted, instructions will be included on sending your quilt for judging. |
| April 9, 2004 | Accepted quilts must be received by the American Quilter's Society, 5801 Kentucky Dam Road, Paducah, KY 42003. |
| April 20, 2004 | Awards will be presented at the Awards Banquet (Tuesday evening, April 20) or mailed to those unable to attend. |

Twenty-four hour security will be provided.